THE 30-MINUTE SHAKESPEARE
MACBETH

"Nick Newlin's work as a teaching artist for Folger Education during the past thirteen years has provided students, regardless of their experience with Shakespeare or being on stage, a unique opportunity to tread the boards at the Folger Theatre. Working with students to edit Shakespeare's plays for performance at the annual Folger Shakespeare Festivals has enabled students to gain new insights into the Bard's plays, build their skills of comprehension and critical reading, and just plain have fun working collaboratively with their peers.

Folger Education promotes performance-based teaching of Shakespeare's plays, providing students with an interactive approach to Shakespeare's plays in which they participate in a close reading of the text through intellectual, physical, and vocal engagement. Newlin's *The 30-Minute Shakespeare* series is an invaluable resource for teachers of Shakespeare, and for all who are interested in performing the plays."

ROBERT YOUNG, PH.D.
DIRECTOR OF EDUCATION
FOLGER SHAKESPEARE LIBRARY

Macbeth: The 30-Minute Shakespeare
ISBN 978-1-935550-02-0
Adaptation, essays, and notes © 2010 by Nick Newlin

There is no royalty for performing *Macbeth: The 30-Minute Shakespeare* in a
classroom or on a stage; however, permission must be obtained for all playscripts
used by the actors. The publisher hereby grants unlimited photocopy permission
for one series of performances to all acting groups that have purchased at least
five (5) copies of the paperback edition, or one (1) copy of the downloadable
PDF edition available for $12.95 from www.30MinuteShakespeare.com.

Cover design by Sarah Juckniess
Printed in the United States of America

Distributed by Consortium Book Sales & Distribution
www.cbsd.com

NICOLO WHIMSEY PRESS
www.30MinuteShakespeare.com

Art Director: Sarah Juckniess
Managing Editor: Katherine Little

THE TRAGEDIE of

MACBETH

THE 30-MINUTE SHAKESPEARE

Written by **WILLIAM SHAKESPEARE**

Abridged AND Edited
by **NICK NEWLIN**

Nicolo Whimsey Press
Press

Brandywine, MD

To my Dad,
Bill Newlin—
a wonderful
role model

Special thanks to Joanne Flynn, Bill Newlin, Eliza Newlin
Carney, William and Louisa Newlin, Michael Tolaydo, Hilary
Kacser, Sarah Juckniess, Katherine Little, Eva Zimmerman,
Julie Schaper and all of Consortium, Leo Bowman and the
students, faculty, and staff at Banneker Academic High School,
and Robert Young Ph.D., and the Folger Shakespeare Library,
especially the wonderful Education Department.

✳ TABLE OF CONTENTS

✳ NO EXPERIENCE NECESSARY

I was not a big "actor type" in high school, so if you weren't either, or if the young people you work with are not, then this book is for you. Whether or not you work with "actor types," you can use this book to stage a lively and captivating thirty-minute version of a Shakespeare play. No experience is necessary.

When I was about eleven years old, my parents took me to see Shakespeare's *Two Gentlemen of Verona*, which was being performed as a Broadway musical. I didn't comprehend every word I heard, but I was enthralled with the language, the characters, and the story, and I understood enough of it to follow along. From then on, I associated Shakespeare with *fun*.

Of course Shakespeare is fun. The Elizabethan audiences knew it, which is one reason he was so popular. It didn't matter that some of the language eluded them. The characters were passionate and vibrant, and their conflicts were compelling. Young people study Shakespeare in high school, but more often than not they read his work like a text book and then get quizzed on academic elements of the play, such as plot, theme, and vocabulary. These are all very interesting, but not nearly as interesting as standing up and performing a scene! It is through performance that the play comes alive and all its "academic" elements are revealed. There is nothing more satisfying to a student or teacher than the feeling of "owning" a Shakespeare play, and that can only come from performing it.

But Shakespeare's plays are often two or more hours long, making the performance of an entire play almost out of the question. One can perform a single scene, which is certainly a good start, but what about the story? What about the changes a character goes through as the play progresses? When school groups perform one scene unedited, or when they lump several plays together, the audience can get lost. This is why I have always preferred to tell the story of the play.

The 30-Minute Shakespeare gives students and teachers a chance to get up on their feet and act out a Shakespeare play in half an hour, using his language. The emphasis is on key scenes, with narrative bridges between scenes to keep the audience caught up on the action. The stage directions are built into this script so that young actors do not have to stand in one place; they can move and tell the story with their actions as well as their words. And it can all be done in a classroom during class time!

That is where this book was born: not in a research library, a graduate school lecture, a professional stage, or even an after-school drama club. All of the play cuttings in *The 30-Minute Shakespeare* were first rehearsed in a D.C. public high school English class, and performed successfully at the Folger Shakespeare Library's annual Secondary School Shakespeare Festival. The players were not necessarily "actor types." For many of them, this was their first performance in a play.

Something almost miraculous happens when students perform Shakespeare. They "get" it. By occupying the characters and speaking the words out loud, students gain a level of understanding and appreciation that is unachievable by simply reading the text. That is the magic of a performance-based method of learning Shakespeare, and this book makes the formerly daunting task of staging a Shakespeare play possible for anybody.

With *The 30-Minute Shakespeare* book series I hope to help teachers and students produce a Shakespeare play in a short amount of time, thus jump-starting the process of discovering the beauty, magic, and fun of the Bard. Plot, theme, and language reveal themselves through the performance of these half-hour play cuttings, and everybody involved receives the priceless gift of "owning" a piece of Shakespeare. The result is an experience that is fun and engaging, and one that we can all carry with us as we play out our own lives on the stages of the world.

NICK NEWLIN
Brandywine, MD
March 2010

CHARACTERS IN THE PLAY

The following is a list of characters that appear in this cutting of Macbeth.

Sixteen actors performed in the original production. This number can be increased to about thirty or decreased to about twelve by having actors share or double roles.

For the full breakdown of characters, see Sample Program.

FIRST WITCH

SECOND WITCH

THIRD WITCH

MACBETH: A Scottish general, Thane of Glamis

BANQUO: A general, prophesied by witches to inherit throne

ROSS: A Scottish nobleman

DUNCAN: King of Scotland

MALCOLM: son of King Duncan

LADY MACBETH: Macbeth's ambitious wife

MURDERER

LENNOX: A Scottish nobleman

GENTLEWOMAN

DOCTOR

MACDUFF: A Scottish nobleman, hostile to Macbeth's kingship

NARRATORS

✳ **SCENE 1.** (ACT I, SCENES I AND II)

A desert place.

SOUND OPERATOR *plays* Sound Cue #1 *("Intro music, thunder, and lightning").*

Enter **THREE WITCHES** *from stage rear, talking.*

FIRST WITCH
> When shall we three meet again
> In thunder, lightning, or in rain?

SECOND WITCH
> When the hurlyburly's done,
> When the battle's lost and won.

THIRD WITCH
> That will be ere the set of sun.

ALL
> Fair is foul, and foul is fair:
> Hover through the fog and filthy air.

SOUND OPERATOR *plays* Sound Cue #2 *("Drum").*

THIRD WITCH
> A drum, a drum!
> Macbeth doth come.

ALL *(circling, around)*
> The weird sisters, hand in hand,

Posters of the sea and land,
Thus do go about, about:
Peace! the charm's wound up.

Enter MACBETH *and* BANQUO *from stage right.*

MACBETH

So foul and fair a day I have not seen.

BANQUO

What are these
So wither'd and so wild in their attire,
That look not like the inhabitants o' the earth,
And yet are on't?

MACBETH

Speak, if you can: what are you?

FIRST WITCH *(bowing)*

All hail, Macbeth! hail to thee, thane of Glamis!

SECOND WITCH *(bowing)*

All hail, Macbeth, hail to thee, thane of Cawdor!

THIRD WITCH *(bowing)*

All hail, Macbeth, thou shalt be king hereafter!
(to BANQUO*)* Thou shalt get kings, though thou be none:
So all hail, Macbeth and Banquo!

FIRST WITCH

Banquo and Macbeth, all hail!

MACBETH

Stay, you imperfect speakers, tell me more:
I know I am thane of Glamis;
But how of Cawdor? the thane of Cawdor lives,

and to be king
Stands not within the prospect of belief,
Speak, I charge you.

Exit WITCHES, *vanishing in all directions.*

BANQUO *(moving center stage, with* MACBETH*)*
Whither are they vanish'd?

MACBETH
Into the air; As breath into the wind.
(to BANQUO*)* Your children shall be kings.

BANQUO
You shall be king.

MACBETH
And thane of Cawdor too: went it not so?

BANQUO
Who's here?

Enter ROSS *from stage right.*

ROSS
The king hath happily received, Macbeth,
The news of thy success; He bade me, from him, call
thee thane of Cawdor:

BANQUO
What, can the devil speak true?

MACBETH
(aside) I am thane of Cawdor:
If chance will have me king, why, chance may crown me,
Without my stir.

(to all) Let us toward the king.
Think upon what hath chanced, and, at more time,
The interim having weigh'd it, let us speak
Our free hearts each to other.

BANQUO

Very gladly.

MACBETH

Till then, enough. Come, friends.

Exit all, following MACBETH.

STAGEHAND *moves throne center stage.*

Enter NARRATOR *from stage right.*

✳ SCENE 2. (ACT I, SCENES IV AND V)

The palace.

NARRATOR
> King Duncan thanks Macbeth and Banquo for
> their heroics, and announces his intention to have
> his son Malcolm succeed him as King. Macbeth is
> convinced that he can only become King by killing
> King Duncan.

Exit **NARRATOR** *stage rear.*

Enter **DUNCAN** *and* **MALCOLM** *from stage rear, standing by throne. Enter* **MACBETH** *and* **BANQUO** *from stage left.* **DUNCAN** *shakes* **MACBETH'S** *hand and sits in throne.*

DUNCAN
> O worthiest cousin!
> More is thy due than more than all can pay.

MACBETH *(bowing to* **KING DUNCAN***)*
> The service and the loyalty I owe,
> In doing it, pays itself. Your highness' part
> Is to receive our duties; and our duties
> Are to your throne and children
> by doing every thing
> Safe toward your love and honour.

DUNCAN
> Welcome hither:

I have begun to plant thee, and will labour
To make thee full of growing. Noble Banquo,
That hast no less deserved, let me enfold thee
And hold thee to my heart.

BANQUO (*bowing*)
There if I grow,
The harvest is your own.

DUNCAN
We will establish our estate upon
Our eldest, Malcolm, whom we name hereafter
The Prince of Cumberland;

MACBETH
(*aside*) The Prince of Cumberland! that is a step
On which I must fall down, or else o'erleap,
For in my way it lies. Stars, hide your fires;
Let not light see my black and deep desires:
The eye wink at the hand; yet let that be,
Which the eye fears, when it is done, to see.

Exit MACBETH *stage right.*

DUNCAN (*to* BANQUO)
True, worthy Banquo; he is full so valiant,
Let's after him.

Exit DUNCAN *and* BANQUO, *following* MACBETH *stage right.*

STAGEHAND ONE *removes throne.* STAGEHAND TWO *places chair stage left, slightly downstage.*

Enter NARRATOR *from stage left.*

✳ SCENE 3. (ACT II, SCENES I AND II)

Inverness, Macbeth's castle.

NARRATOR
> Lady Macbeth reads her husband's letter about his meeting with the Witches. Macbeth arrives, and she tells him that she will take charge of the preparations for King Duncan's murder.

Exit **NARRATOR** *stage rear.*

Enter **LADY MACBETH** *from stage right, reading a letter. She sits in chair stage left.*

LADY MACBETH *(reading)*
> "Came missives from the king, who
> all-hailed me 'Thane of Cawdor'; by which title,
> before, these weird sisters saluted me, and referred
> me to the coming on of time, with 'Hail, king that
> shalt be!' This have I thought good to deliver
> thee, my dearest partner of greatness."
> *(speaking now, and standing)* Glamis thou art, and
> Cawdor; and shalt be
> What thou art promised: yet do I fear thy nature;
> It is too full o' the milk of human kindness
> Hie thee hither, *(stands behind chair as if she is
>   standing over* **MACBETH***)*
> That I may pour my spirits in thine ear;
> And chastise with the valour of my tongue
> All that impedes thee from the golden round,

(pretends to set a crown on his head)
Which fate and metaphysical aid doth seem
To have thee crown'd withal.
The king comes here to-night.
He brings great news.
The raven himself is hoarse
That croaks the fatal entrance of Duncan
Under my battlements.
(walks downstage center; beckons with arms) Come,
you spirits
That tend on mortal thoughts, unsex me here,
And fill me from the crown to the toe top-full
Of direst cruelty! make thick my blood;
Stop up the access and passage to remorse,
(turns downstage right) Come, thick night,
And pall thee in the dunnest smoke of hell,
That my keen knife see not the wound it makes,
Nor heaven peep through the blanket of the dark,
To cry "Hold, hold!"

Enter MACBETH *from stage right.* LADY MACBETH *goes to greet him, excited to see him, and kisses his hand. She leads him to the chair downstage left.*

Great Glamis! worthy Cawdor!
Thy letters have transported me beyond
This ignorant present, and I feel now
The future in the instant.

MACBETH *(not yet sitting, turns to her)*
My dearest love,
Duncan comes here to-night.

LADY MACBETH
And when goes hence?

MACBETH
> To-morrow, as he purposes.

LADY MACBETH
> O, never
> Shall sun that morrow see!
> Your face, my thane, is as a book where men
> May read strange matters.
> *(sits* MACBETH *in chair and looks at him)* Look like the
> > innocent flower,
> But be the serpent under't. He that's coming
> Must be provided for: and you shall put
> This night's great business into my dispatch;
> Which shall to all our nights and days to come
> Give solely sovereign sway and masterdom.

MACBETH
> We will speak further.

LADY MACBETH
> Only look up clear;
> To alter favour ever is to fear:
> Leave all the rest to me.

Exit LADY MACBETH *stage rear.*

MACBETH *(still sitting in chair; sees dagger in front of him)*
> Is this a dagger which I see before me,
> The handle toward my hand? Come, let me clutch thee.
> > *(tries to clutch dagger, but it has no substance)*
> I have thee not, and yet I see thee still.
> Art thou not, fatal vision, sensible
> To feeling as to sight? or art thou but
> A dagger of the mind, a false creation,
> Proceeding from the heat-oppressed brain?
> I see thee yet, in form as palpable

As this which now I draw. *(draws his own dagger
    from belt)*
Thou marshall'st me the way that I was going;
And such an instrument I was to use.
Thou sure and firm-set earth,
Hear not my steps, which way they walk, for fear
Thy very stones prate of my whereabout.

SOUND OPERATOR *plays* Sound Cue #3 *("Bell ring")*.

I go, and it is done; the bell invites me.
Hear it not, Duncan; for it is a knell
That summons thee to heaven or to hell.

Exit MACBETH *stage rear. Enter* LADY MACBETH *from stage left.*

LADY MACBETH
That which hath made them drunk hath made me bold;
What hath quench'd them hath given me fire.
I have drugg'd their possets,
That death and nature do contend about them,
Whether they live or die.

SOUND OPERATOR *plays* Sound Cue #4 *("Shrieking owl")*.

Hark! Peace!
It was the owl that shriek'd,

Enter MACBETH *from stage rear. His hands are bloody and he
holds two bloody daggers.*

My husband!

MACBETH
I have done the deed. Didst thou not hear a noise?

LADY MACBETH
> I heard the owl scream and the crickets cry.

MACBETH *(looking at his hands)*
> This is a sorry sight.

LADY MACBETH *(grabs him by the shoulders to calm him down)*
> A foolish thought, to say a sorry sight.

MACBETH
> Methought I heard a voice cry "Sleep no more!
> Macbeth does murder sleep"—the innocent sleep,
> Sleep that knits up the ravell'd sleeve of care,
> "Macbeth shall sleep no more."

LADY MACBETH
> Who was it that thus cried? Why, worthy thane,
> You do unbend your noble strength, to think
> So brainsickly of things. *(notices daggers)*
> Why did you bring these daggers from the place?
> They must lie there: go carry them; and smear
> The sleepy grooms with blood. *(pushes him back
>   toward door)*

MACBETH *(resists her pushing and becomes more agitated)*
> I'll go no more:
> I am afraid to think what I have done;
> Look on't again I dare not.

LADY MACBETH
> Infirm of purpose! *(takes daggers from him)*
> Give me the daggers: the sleeping and the dead
> Are but as pictures: 'tis the eye of childhood
> That fears a painted devil. If he do bleed,
> I'll gild the faces of the grooms withal;
> For it must seem their guilt.

Exit LADY MACBETH *stage rear.*

SOUND OPERATOR *plays* Sound Cue #5 *("Knocking").*

MACBETH
> Whence is that knocking?
> How is't with me, when every noise appals me?
> *(looks at his hands)*
> What hands are here? ha! they pluck out mine eyes.
> Will all great Neptune's ocean wash this blood
> Clean from my hand?

Re-enter LADY MACBETH.

LADY MACBETH
> My hands are of your colour; but I shame
> To wear a heart so white.

SOUND OPERATOR *plays* Sound Cue #6 *("Knocking").*

MACBETH
> To know my deed, 'twere best not know myself.

SOUND OPERATOR *plays* Sound Cue #7 *("Knocking").*

> Wake Duncan with thy knocking! I would thou
> couldst!

Exit MACBETH *and* LADY MACBETH *stage left, hurriedly.*

STAGEHAND ONE *brings on two chairs;* STAGEHAND TWO *brings on one chair.* STAGEHANDS THREE AND FOUR *bring on table and arrange four chairs around it.*

Enter NARRATOR *from stage right, coming downstage.*

✳ SCENE 4. (ACT V, SCENE IV)

Hall in the palace.

NARRATOR
Having ordered Banquo murdered, Macbeth discovers an unexpected guest at his feast: Banquo's ghost!

Exit **NARRATOR** *stage rear.*

A banquet prepared. Enter **MACBETH, LADY MACBETH, ROSS,** *and* **LENNOX.**

MACBETH *(gesturing)*
Sit down and hearty welcome.

ROSS
Thanks to your majesty.

MURDERER *appears at the door, stage right.*

MACBETH *(approaching the door; to* **MURDERER***)*
There's blood on thy face.

MURDERER
'Tis Banquo's then.

MACBETH
'Tis better thee without than he within.
Is he dispatch'd?

MURDERER

> My lord, his throat is cut.

MACBETH

> And Fleance?

MURDERER

> Most royal sir,
> Fleance is 'scaped.

MACBETH

> Now I am, confined, in
> saucy doubts and fears. But Banquo's safe?

MURDERER

> Ay, my good lord: safe in a ditch he bides,
> With twenty trenched gashes on his head.

MACBETH

> Thanks for that:
> Get thee gone:

Exit MURDERER *stage right.*

LADY MACBETH

> My royal lord,
> You do not give the cheer;

MACBETH *(toasting)*
> Now, good digestion
> And health!

ALL *at table toast and give a cheer.*

LENNOX

> May't please your highness sit.

Enter the GHOST OF BANQUO *from stage left. He sits at the table with his back to audience.*

MACBETH
> The table's full.

LENNOX
> Here is a place reserved, sir.

MACBETH
> Where?

GHOST OF BANQUO *points at* MACBETH.

LENNOX
> Here, my good lord. What is't that moves your
> highness?

MACBETH
> Which of you have done this?

ROSS
> What, my good lord?

MACBETH
> Thou canst not say I did it: Never shake
> Thy gory locks at me.

ROSS
> Gentlemen, rise: his highness is not well.

LADY MACBETH
> Sit, worthy friends: my lord is often thus,
> And hath been from his youth: pray you, keep seat;
> *(to* MACBETH, *aside)* Are you a man?

MACBETH

>Ay, and a bold one, that dare look on that
>Which might appal the devil.

LADY MACBETH

>O proper stuff!
>This is the very painting of your fear:
>This is the air-drawn dagger which, you said,
>Led you to Duncan.
>Why do you make such faces? When all's done,
>You look but on a stool.

GHOST OF BANQUO *points at* MACBETH *again.*

MACBETH (*terrified*)

>Behold! look! lo!

LADY MACBETH

>My worthy lord,
>Your noble friends do lack you.

MACBETH

>Do not muse at me, my most worthy friends,
>I have a strange infirmity, which is nothing
>To those that know me. Come, love and health to all;
>Then I'll sit down. I drink to our dear friend
>   Banquo, whom we miss;

GHOST OF BANQUO *points again.*

MACBETH

>Quit my sight! let the earth hide thee!
>Thy bones are marrowless, thy blood is cold;
>Thou hast no speculation in those eyes
>Which thou dost glare with! Hence, horrible shadow!
>Unreal mockery, hence!

Exit GHOST OF BANQUO *stage left, still looking and/or pointing at* MACBETH.

> Why, so: being gone,
> I am a man again.
> *(to* GUESTS, *who are starting to get up to leave)* Pray
> you, sit still.

LADY MACBETH

> You have displaced the mirth
> With most admired disorder.

ROSS

> What sights, my lord?

LADY MACBETH

> I pray you, speak not; he grows worse and worse;
> Go at once.

LENNOX

> Good night; and better health
> Attend his majesty!

LADY MACBETH

> A kind good night to all!

Exit all but MACBETH *and* LADY MACBETH, *stage left.*

MACBETH

> It will have blood; they say, blood will have blood:
> Stones have been known to move and trees to speak;
> I will, to the weird sisters:
> More shall they speak; for now I am bent to know,
> By the worst means, the worst. For mine own good,
> I am in blood.

Strange things I have in head, that will to hand;
Which must be acted ere they may be scann'd.

LADY MACBETH

You lack the season of all natures, sleep.

MACBETH

Come, we'll to sleep.
We are yet but young in deed.

Exit MACBETH *and* LADY MACBETH *stage left.*

STAGEHANDS ONE AND TWO *remove four chairs.* STAGEHANDS
THREE AND FOUR *remove table.*

Enter NARRATOR *from stage right, coming downstage.*

✳ SCENE 5. (ACT IV, SCENE I)

A cavern.

Enter THREE WITCHES *from stage rear, one bringing on cauldron and setting it center stage.*

NARRATOR
> The Three Witches conjure around the cauldron, making predictions that embolden Macbeth, who decides to kill Macduff's family.

Exit NARRATOR *stage rear.*

SOUND OPERATOR *plays* Sound Cue #8 *("Thunder").*

FIRST WITCH
> Thrice the brinded cat hath mew'd.

SECOND WITCH
> Thrice and once the hedge-pig whined.

THIRD WITCH
> Harpier cries 'Tis time, 'tis time.

FIRST WITCH
> Round about the cauldron go;
> In the poison'd entrails throw.
> Swelter'd venom sleeping got,
> Boil thou first i' the charmed pot.

ALL

> Double, double toil and trouble;
> Fire burn, and cauldron bubble.

SECOND WITCH

> Fillet of a fenny snake,
> In the cauldron boil and bake;
> Eye of newt and toe of frog,
> Wool of bat and tongue of dog,
> For a charm of powerful trouble,
> Like a hell-broth boil and bubble.

ALL

> Double, double toil and trouble;
> Fire burn and cauldron bubble.

THIRD WITCH

> Liver of blaspheming Jew,
> Gall of goat, and slips of yew
> Finger of birth-strangled babe
> Ditch-deliver'd by a drab,
> Make the gruel thick and slab:
> Add thereto a tiger's chaudron,
> For the ingredients of our cauldron.

ALL

> Double, double toil and trouble;
> Fire burn and cauldron bubble.

SECOND WITCH

> Cool it with a baboon's blood,
> Then the charm is firm and good.
> By the pricking of my thumbs,
> Something wicked this way comes.
> Open, locks,
> Whoever knocks!

THREE WITCHES *scatter across the stage, all facing a point above the*
audience's head, center, where the "apparitions" are appearing.

Enter MACBETH *from stage right.*

MACBETH
> How now, you secret, black, and midnight hags!
> What is't you do?

ALL
> A deed without a name.

MACBETH
> I conjure you, by that which you profess,
> Howe'er you come to know it, answer me:

SOUND OPERATOR *plays* Sound Cue #9 *("Thunder").*

THREE WITCHES *and* MACBETH *look at spot in space where First*
Apparition, an armed Head, appears.

FIRST WITCH
> Macbeth! Macbeth! Macbeth! beware Macduff;
> Beware the thane of Fife.

SOUND OPERATOR *plays* Sound Cue #10 *("Thunder").*

Second Apparition, a bloody Child, appears.

SECOND WITCH
> Macbeth! Macbeth! Macbeth!

MACBETH
> Had I three ears, I'ld hear thee.

SECOND WITCH
> Be bloody, bold, and resolute; laugh to scorn

The power of man, for none of woman born
Shall harm Macbeth.

MACBETH

Then live, Macduff: what need I fear of thee?
But yet I'll make assurance double sure, thou shalt
    not live.

SOUND OPERATOR *plays* Sound Cue #11 *("Thunder").*

*Third Apparition, a Child crowned, with a tree in his hand,
appears.*

THIRD WITCH

Macbeth shall never vanquish'd be until
Great Birnam wood to high Dunsinane hill
Shall come against him.

MACBETH

That will never be
Who can impress the forest, bid the tree
Unfix his earth-bound root? Sweet bodements!
Good!

SOUND OPERATOR *plays* Sound Cue #12 *("Witches' Music").*

THREE WITCHES *dance and then exit, vanishing.*

MACBETH

Where are they? Gone?

Enter LENNOX *from stage right.*

LENNOX

What's your grace's will?

MACBETH

> Saw you the weird sisters?

LENNOX

> No, my lord.
> My lord, Macduff is fled to England.

MACBETH

> The castle of Macduff I will surprise;
> Seize upon Fife; give to the edge o' the sword
> His wife, his babes, and all unfortunate souls
> That trace him in his line.

Exit MACBETH *and* LENNOX *stage left.*

STAGEHAND ONE *removes cauldron.* STAGEHAND TWO *sets small table (as a sink) downstage and slightly left.*

Enter NARRATOR *from stage right, coming downstage center.*

✳ SCENE 6. (ACT V, SCENE I)

Dunsinane. Anteroom in the castle.

NARRATOR

> A gentlewoman who waits on Lady Macbeth calls on a doctor to witness Lady Macbeth's compulsive sleepwalking behavior.

Exit **NARRATOR** *stage rear.*

Enter **DOCTOR** *and* **GENTLEWOMAN** *from stage right. Enter* **LADY MACBETH***, with a candle, from stage left.*

GENTLEWOMAN

> Lo you, here she comes! This is her very guise; and, upon my life, fast asleep.

DOCTOR

> How came she by that light?

GENTLEWOMAN

> She has light by her continually; 'tis her command.

DOCTOR

> You see, her eyes are open.

GENTLEWOMAN

> Ay, but their sense is shut.

DOCTOR

>What is it she does now? Look, how she rubs her hands.

GENTLEWOMAN

>It is an accustomed action with her, to seem thus washing her hands:

LADY MACBETH

>Yet here's a spot.
>Out, damned spot! out, I say!—One: two:
>Who would have thought the old man
>>to have had so much blood in him.
>The thane of Fife had a wife: where is she now?—
>What, will these hands ne'er be clean?

DOCTOR (*to* GENTLEWOMAN)

>You have known what you should not.

GENTLEWOMAN

>She has spoke what she should not, I am sure of that: heaven knows what she has known.

LADY MACBETH

>Here's the smell of the blood still: all the perfumes of Arabia will not sweeten this little hand. Oh, oh, oh!

DOCTOR

>What a sigh is there! The heart is sorely charged.

GENTLEWOMAN

>I would not have such a heart in my bosom for the dignity of the whole body.

LADY MACBETH

>Wash your hands,

Banquo's buried;
He cannot come out on's grave.
To bed, to bed! there's knocking at the gate:
come, come, come, come, give me your hand. What's
done cannot be undone.—To bed, to bed, to bed!

Exit LADY MACBETH *stage left.*

DOCTOR

Foul whisperings are abroad: unnatural deeds
Do breed unnatural troubles: infected minds
To their deaf pillows will discharge their secrets:
God, God forgive us all! Look after her;
I think, but dare not speak.

GENTLEWOMAN

Good night, good doctor.

Exit DOCTOR *and* GENTLEWOMAN *stage right.*

STAGEHAND *removes table.*

Enter NARRATOR *from stage right, coming downstage center.*

✳ SCENE 7. (ACT V, SCENE VIII)

Another part of the field.

NARRATOR

Macbeth and Macduff fight fiercely, as the Witches' prophecies unfold.

Exit **NARRATOR** *stage rear.*

Enter **MACBETH***, armed, from stage right.*

MACBETH

Why should I play the Roman fool, and die
On mine own sword?

Enter **MACDUFF** *from stage left.*

MACDUFF

Turn, hell-hound, turn!

They fight.

MACBETH

Thou losest labour:
I bear a charmed life, which must not yield,
To one of woman born.

MACDUFF

Despair thy charm;
And let the angel whom thou still hast served

Tell thee, Macduff was from his mother's womb
Untimely ripp'd.

MACBETH

Accursed be that tongue that tells me so,
For it hath cow'd my better part of man!
I'll not fight with thee.

MACDUFF

Then yield thee, coward,
We'll have thee, as our rarer monsters are,
Painted on a pole, and underwrit,
"Here may you see the tyrant."

MACBETH

I will not yield,
To kiss the ground before young Malcolm's feet,
Though Birnam wood be come to Dunsinane,
And thou opposed, being of no woman born,
Yet I will try the last. Lay on, Macduff,
And damn'd be him that first cries, "Hold, enough!"

MACBETH *and* MACDUFF *exit stage rear, fighting.*

Enter MALCOLM, ROSS, *and* LENNOX *from stage right.*

MALCOLM

I would the friends we miss were safe arrived.
Macduff is missing,
Here comes newer comfort.

Re-enter MACDUFF, *from stage rear, with* MACBETH'S *head in a bag.*

MACDUFF *(to Malcolm)*

Hail, king! for so thou art: behold, where stands

The usurper's cursed head: the time is free:
Hail, King of Scotland!

ALL

Hail, King of Scotland!

During MALCOLM'S *speech, all cast members re-enter and form a semicircle.*

MALCOLM

What's more to do,
Producing forth the cruel ministers
Of this dead butcher and his fiend-like queen,
Who, as 'tis thought, by self and violent hands
Took off her life;
This, we will perform in measure, time and place:
So, thanks to all at once and to each one,
Whom we invite to see us crown'd at Scone.

ALL

Out, out, brief candle!
Life's but a walking shadow, a poor player
That struts and frets his hour upon the stage
And then is heard no more: it is a tale
Told by an idiot, full of sound and fury,
Signifying nothing.

All hold hands and take a bow. Exeunt.

✳ PERFORMING SHAKESPEARE

HOW *THE 30-MINUTE SHAKESPEARE* WAS BORN

In 1981 I performed a "Shakespeare Juggling" piece called "To Juggle or Not To Juggle" at the first Folger Library Secondary School Shakespeare Festival. The audience consisted of about 200 Washington, D.C. area high school students who had just performed thirty-minute versions of Shakespeare plays for each other and were jubilant over the experience. I was dressed in a jester's outfit, and my job was to entertain them. I juggled and jested and played with Shakespeare's words, notably Hamlet's "To be or not to be" soliloquy, to very enthusiastic response. I was struck by how much my "Shakespeare Juggling" resonated with a group who had just performed Shakespeare themselves. "Getting" Shakespeare is a heady feeling, especially for adolescents, and I am continually delighted at how much joy and satisfaction young people derive from performing Shakespeare. Simply reading and studying this great playwright does not even come close to inspiring the kind of enthusiasm that comes from performance.

Surprisingly, many of these students were not "actor types." A good percentage of the students performing Shakespeare that day were part of an English class which had rehearsed the plays during class time. Fifteen years later, when I first started directing plays in D.C. public schools as a Teaching Artist with the Folger Shakespeare Library, I entered a ninth grade English class as a guest and spent two or three days a week for two or three months preparing students for the Folger's annual Secondary School Shakespeare Festival. I have conducted this annual residency with the Folger ever since. Every year for seven action-packed days, eight groups of students between grades seven and twelve tread the boards onstage at the Folger's Elizabethan Theatre, a grand recreation of a sixteenth-century venue with a three-tiered gallery, carved oak columns, and a sky-painted canopy.

As noted on the Folger website (www.folger.edu), "The festival is a celebration of the Bard, not a competition. Festival commentators—drawn from the professional theater and Shakespeare education communities—recognize exceptional performances, student directors, and good spirit amongst the students with selected awards at the end of each day. They are also available to share feedback with the students."

My annual Folger Teaching Artist engagement, directing a Shakespeare play in a public high school English class, is the most challenging and the most rewarding thing I do all year. I hope this book can bring you the same rewards.

GETTING STARTED

GAMES

How can you get an English class (or any other group of young people, or even adults) to start the seemingly daunting task of performing a Shakespeare play? You have already successfully completed the critical first step, which is buying this book. You hold in your hand a performance-ready, thirty-minute cutting of a Shakespeare play, with stage directions to get the actors moving about the stage purposefully. But it's a good idea to warm the group up with some theater games.

One good initial exercise is called "Positive/Negative Salutations." Students stand in two lines facing each other (four or five students in each line) and, reading from index cards, greet each other, first with a "Positive" salutation in Shakespeare's language (using actual phrases from the plays), followed by a "negative" greeting.

Additionally, short vocal exercises are an essential part of the preparation process. The following is a very simple and effective vocal warm-up: Beginning with the number two, have the whole group count to twenty using increments of two (i.e., "Two, four, six . . ."). Increase the volume slightly with each number, reaching top volume with "twenty," and then decrease the volume while counting back down, so that the students are practically whispering when they arrive again at "two." This exercise teaches dynamics and allows them to get loud as a group without any individual pressure. Frequently during a rehearsal period, if a student is mumbling inaudibly, I will refer back to this exercise as a reminder that we can and often do belt it out!

"Stomping Words" is a game that is very helpful at getting a handle on Shakespeare's rhythm. Choose a passage in iambic pentameter and have the group members walk around the room in a circle, stomping their feet on the second beat of each line:

Two **house**-holds, **both** a-**like** in **dig**-nity
In **fair** Ve-**rona Where** we **lay** our **scene**

Do the same thing with a prose passage, and have the students discuss their experience with it, including points at which there is an extra beat, etc., and what, if anything, it might signify.

I end every vocal warm-up with a group reading of one of the speeches from the play, emphasizing diction and projection, bouncing off consonants, and encouraging the group members to listen to each other so that they can speak the lines together in unison. For variety I will throw in some classic "tongue twisters" too, such as, "The sixth sheik's sixth sheep is sick."

The Folger Shakespeare Library's website (http://www.folger.edu) and their book series *Shakespeare Set Free*, edited by Peggy O'Brien, are two great resources for getting started with a performance-based teaching of Shakespeare in the classroom. The Folger website has numerous helpful resources and activities, many submitted by teachers, for helping a class actively participate in the process of getting to know a Shakespeare play. For more simple theater games, Viola Spolin's *Theatre Games for the Classroom* is very helpful, as is one I use frequently, *Theatre Games for Young Performers*.

HATS AND PROPS

Introducing a few hats and props early in the process is a good way to get the action going. Hats, in particular, provide a nice avenue for giving young actors a non-verbal way of getting into character. In the opening weeks, when students are still holding onto their scripts, a hat can give an actor a way to "feel" like a character. Young actors are natural masters at injecting their own personality into what they wear, and even small choices made with how a hat is worn (jauntily, shadily, cockily, mysteriously) provide a starting point for discussion of specific characters, their traits, and their relationships with other characters. All such discussions always lead back to one thing: the text. "Mining the text" is consistently the best strategy for uncovering the mystery of Shakespeare's language. That is where all the answers lie: in the words themselves.

WHAT DO THE WORDS MEAN?

It is essential that young actors know what they are saying when they recite Shakespeare. If not, they might as well be scat singing, riffing on sounds and rhythm but not conveying a specific meaning. The real question is: What do the words mean? The answer is multifaceted, and can be found in more than one place. The New Folger Library paperback editions of the plays themselves (edited by Barbara Mowat and Paul Werstine, Washington Square Press) are a great resource for understanding Shakespeare's words and passages and "translating" them into modern English. These editions also contain chapters on Shakespeare's language, his life, his theater, a "Modern Perspective," and further reading. There is a wealth of scholarship embedded in these wonderful books, and I make it a point to read them cover to cover before embarking on a play-directing project. At the very least, it is a good idea for any adult who intends to direct a Shakespeare play with a group of students to go through the explanatory notes that appear on the pages facing the text. These explanatory notes are an indispensable "translation tool."

The best way to get students to understand what Shakespeare's words mean is to ask them what they think they mean. Students have their own associations with the words and with how they sound and feel. The best ideas on how to perform Shakespeare often come directly from the students, not from anybody else's notion. If a student has an idea or feeling about a word or passage, and it resonates with her emotionally, physically, or spiritually, then Shakespeare's words can be a vehicle for her feelings. That can result in some powerful performances!

I make it my job as director to read the explanatory notes in the Folger text, but I make it clear to the students that almost "anything goes" when trying to understand Shakespeare. There are no wrong interpretations. Students have their own experiences, with some shared and some uniquely their own. If someone has an association with the phrase "canker-blossom," or if the words make that student or his character feel or act a certain way, then that is the "right" way to decipher it.

I encourage the students to refer to the Folger text's explanatory notes and to keep a pocket dictionary handy. Young actors must attach some meaning to every word or line they recite. If I feel an actor is glossing over a word, I will stop him and ask him what he is saying. If he doesn't know, we will figure it out together as a group.

PROCESS VS. PRODUCT

The process of learning Shakespeare by performing one of his plays is more important than whether everybody remembers his lines or whether somebody misses a cue or an entrance. But my Teaching Artist residencies have always had the end goal of a public performance for about 200 other students, so naturally the performance starts to take precedence over the process somewhere around dress rehearsal in the students' minds. It is my job to make sure the actors are prepared—otherwise they will remember the embarrassing moment of a public mistake and not the glorious triumph of owning a Shakespeare play.

In one of my earlier years of play directing, I was sitting in the audience as one of my narrators stood frozen on stage for at least a minute, trying to remember her opening line. I started scrambling in my backpack below my seat for a script, at last prompting her from the audience. Despite her fine performance, that embarrassing moment is all she remembered from the whole experience. Since then I have made sure to assign at least one person to prompt from backstage if necessary. Additionally, I inform the entire cast that if somebody is dying alone out there, it is okay to rescue him or her with an offstage prompt.

There is always a certain amount of stage fright that will accompany a performance, especially a public one for an unfamiliar audience. As a director, I live with stage fright as well, even though I am not appearing on stage. The only antidote to this is work and preparation. If a young actor is struggling with her lines, I make sure to arrange for a session where we run lines over the telephone. I try to set up a buddy system so that students can run lines with their peers, and this often works well. But if somebody does not have a "buddy," I will personally make the time to help out myself. As I assure my students from the outset, I am not going to let them fail or embarrass themselves. They need an experienced leader. And if the leader has experience in teaching but not in directing Shakespeare, then he needs this book!

It is a good idea to culminate in a public performance, as opposed to an in-class project, even if it is only for another classroom. Student actors want to show their newfound Shakespearian thespian skills to an outside group, and this goal motivates them to do a good job. In that respect, "product" is important. Another wonderful bonus to performing a play is that it is a unifying group effort. Students learn teamwork. They learn to give focus to another actor when he is speaking, and to play off of other characters. I like to end each performance with the entire cast reciting a passage in unison. This is a powerful ending, one that reaffirms the unity of the group.

SEEING SHAKESPEARE PERFORMED

It is very helpful for young actors to see Shakespeare performed by a group of professionals, whether they are appearing live on stage (preferable but not always possible) or on film. Because an entire play can take up two or more full class periods, time may be an issue. I am fortunate because thanks to a local foundation that underwrites theater education in the schools, I have been able to take my school groups to a Folger Theatre matinee of the play that they are performing. I always pick a play that is being performed locally that season. But not all group leaders are that lucky. Fortunately, there is the Internet, specifically YouTube. A quick YouTube search for "Shakespeare" can unearth thousands of results, many appropriate for the classroom.

The first "Hamlet" result showed an 18-year-old African-American actor on the streets of Camden, New Jersey, delivering a riveting performance of Hamlet's "The play's the thing." The second clip was from *Cat Head Theatre,* an animation of cats performing Hamlet. Of course, YouTube boasts not just alley cats and feline thespians, but also clips by true legends of the stage, such as John Gielgud and Richard Burton. These clips can be saved and shown in classrooms, providing useful inspiration.

One advantage of the amazing variety of clips available on YouTube is that students can witness the wide range of interpretations for any given scene, speech, or character in Shakespeare, thus freeing them from any preconceived notion that there is a "right" way to do it. Furthermore, modern interpretations of the Bard may appeal to those who are put off by the "thees and thous" of Elizabethan speech.

By seeing Shakespeare performed either live or on film, students are able to hear the cadence, rhythm, vocal dynamics, and pronunciation of the language, and they can appreciate the life that other actors breathe into the characters. They get to see the story told dramatically, which inspires them to tell their own version.

PUTTING IT ALL TOGETHER

THE STEPS

After a few sessions of theater games to warm up the group, it's time to begin the process of casting the play. Each play cutting in *The 30-Minute Shakespeare* series includes a cast list and a sample program, demonstrating which parts have been divided. Cast size is generally between twelve and thirty students, with major roles frequently assigned to more than one performer. In other words, one student may play Juliet in the first scene, another in the second scene, and yet another in the third. This will distribute the parts evenly so that there is no "star of the show." Furthermore, this prevents actors from being burdened with too many lines. If I have an actor who is particularly talented or enthusiastic, I will give her a bigger role. It is important to go with the grain—one cast member's enthusiasm can be contagious.

I provide the performer of each shared role with a similar head-piece and/or cape, so that the audience can keep track of the characters. When there are sets of twins, I try to use blue shirts and red shirts, so that the audience has at least a fighting chance of figuring it out! Other than these costume consistencies, I rely on the text and the audience's observance to sort out the doubling of characters. Generally, the audience can follow because we are telling the story.

Some participants are shy and do not wish to speak at all on stage. To these students I assign non-speaking parts and technical roles such as sound operator and stage manager. However, I always get everybody on stage at some point, even if it is just for the final group speech, because I want every group member to experience what it is like to be on a stage as part of an ensemble.

CASTING THE PLAY

Young people can be self-conscious and nervous with "formal" auditions, especially if they have little or no acting experience.

I conduct what I call an "informal" audition process. I hand out a questionnaire asking students if there is any particular role that they desire, whether they play a musical instrument. To get a feel for them as people, I also ask them to list one or two hobbies or interests. Occasionally this will inform my casting decisions. If someone can juggle, and the play has the part of a Fool, that skill may come in handy. Dancing or martial arts abilities can also be applied to roles.

For the auditions, I do not use the cut script. I have students stand and read from the Folger edition of the complete text in order to hear how they fare with the longer passages. I encourage them to breathe and carry their vocal energy all the way to the end of a long line of text. I also urge them to play with diction, projection, modulation, and dynamics, elements of speech that we have worked on in our vocal warm-ups and theater games.

I base my casting choices largely on reading ability, vocal strength, and enthusiasm for the project. If someone has requested a particular role, I try to honor that request. I explain that even with a small part, an actor can create a vivid character that adds a lot to the play. Wide variations in personality types can be utilized: if there are two students cast as Romeo, one brooding and one effusive, I try to put the more brooding Romeo in an early lovelorn scene, and place the effusive Romeo in the balcony scene. Occasionally one gets lucky, and the doubling of characters provides a way to match personality types with different aspects of a character's personality. But also be aware of the potential serendipity of non-traditional casting. For example, I have had one of the smallest students in the class play a powerful Othello. True power comes from within!

Generally, I have more females than males in a class, so women are more likely (and more willing) to play male characters than vice versa.

Rare is the high school boy who is brave enough to play a female character, which is unfortunate because it can reap hilarious results.

GET OUTSIDE HELP

Every time there is a fight scene in one of the plays I am directing, I call on my friend Michael Tolaydo, a professional actor and theater professor at St. Mary's College, who is an expert in all aspects of theater, including fight choreography. Not only does Michael stage the fight, but he does so in a way that furthers the action of the play, highlighting character's traits and bringing out the best in the student actors. Fight choreography must be done by an expert or somebody could get hurt. In the absence of such help, super slow-motion fights are always a safe bet and can be quite effective, especially when accompanied by a soundtrack on the boom box.

During dress rehearsals I invite my friend Hilary Kacser. a Washington-area actor and dialect coach for two decades. Because I bring her in late in the rehearsal process, I have her direct her comments to me, which I then filter and relay to the cast. This avoids confusing the cast with a second set of directions. This caveat only applies to general directorial comments from outside visitors. Comments on specific artistic disciplines such as dance, music, and stage combat can come from the outside experts themselves.

If you work in a school, you might have helpful resources within your own building, such as a music or dance teacher who could contribute their expertise to a scene. If nobody is available in your school, try seeking out a member of the local professional theater. Many local performing artists will be glad to help, and the students are usually thrilled to have a visit from a professional performer.

LET STUDENTS BRING THEMSELVES INTO THE PLAY

The best ideas often come from the students themselves. If a young actor has a notion of how to play a scene, I will always give that idea a try. In a rehearsal of *Henry IV, Part 1*, one traveler jumped into the other's arms when they were robbed. It got a huge laugh. This was something that they did on instinct. We kept that bit for the performance, and it worked wonderfully.

As a director, you have to foster an environment in which that kind of spontaneity can occur. The students have to feel safe to experiment. In the same production of *Henry IV*, Falstaff and Hal invented a little fist bump "secret handshake" to use in the battle scene. The students were having fun and bringing parts of themselves into the play. Shakespeare himself would have approved. When possible I try to err on the side of fun because if the young actors are having fun, then they will commit themselves to the project. The beauty of the language, the story, the characters, and the pathos will follow.

There is a balance to be achieved here, however. In that same production of *Henry IV, Part 1*, the student who played Bardolph was having a great time with her character. She carried a leather wineskin around and offered it up to the other characters in the tavern. It was a prop with which she developed a comic relationship. At the end of our thirty-minute *Henry IV, Part 1*, I added a scene from *Henry IV, Part 2* as a coda: The new King Henry V (formerly Falstaff's drinking and carousing buddy Hal) rejects Falstaff, banishing him from within ten miles of the King. It is a sad and sobering moment, one of the most powerful in the play.

But at the performance, in the middle of the King's rejection speech (played by a female student, and her only speech), Bardolph offered her flask to King Henry and got a big laugh, thus not only upstaging the King but also undermining the seriousness and poignancy of the whole scene. She did not know any better; she was bringing herself to the character as I had been encouraging her to do. But it was inappropriate, and in subsequent seasons, if I foresaw something like that happening as an individual joyfully occupied a character, I attempted to prevent it. Some things we cannot predict. Now I make sure to issue a statement warning against changing any of the blocking on show day, and to watch out for upstaging one's peers.

FOUR FORMS OF ENGAGEMENT: VOCAL, EMOTIONAL, PHYSICAL, AND INTELLECTUAL

When directing a Shakespeare play with a group of students, I always start with the words themselves because the words have the power to engage the emotions, mind, and body. Also, I start with the words in action, as in the previously mentioned exercise, "Positive and Negative Salutations." Students become physically engaged; their bodies react to the images the words evoke. The words have the power to trigger a switch in both the teller and the listener, eliciting both an emotional and physical reaction. I have never heard a student utter the line "Fie! Fie! You counterfeit, you puppet you!" without seeing him change before my eyes. His spine stiffens, his eyes widen, and his fingers point menacingly.

Having used Shakespeare's words to engage the students emotionally and physically, one can then return to the text for a more reflective discussion of what the words mean to us personally. I always make sure to leave at least a few class periods open for discussion of the text, line by line, to ensure that students understand intellectually what they feel viscerally. The advantage to a performance-based teaching of Shakespeare is that by engaging students vocally, emotionally, and physically, it is then much easier to engage them intellectually because they are invested in the words, the characters, and the story. We always start on our feet, and later we sit and talk.

SIX ELEMENTS OF DRAMA: PLOT, CHARACTER, THEME, DICTION, MUSIC, AND SPECTACLE

Over two thousand years ago, Aristotle's *Poetics* outlined six elements of drama, in order of importance: Plot, Character, Theme, Diction, Music, and Spectacle. Because Shakespeare was foremost a playwright, it is helpful to take a brief look at these six elements as they relate to directing a Shakespeare play in the classroom.

PLOT (ACTION)

To Aristotle, plot was the most important element. One of the purposes of *The 30-Minute Shakespeare* is to provide a script that tells Shakespeare's stories, as opposed to concentrating on one scene. In a thirty-minute edit of a Shakespeare play, some plot elements are necessarily omitted. For the sake of a full understanding of the characters' relationships and motivations, it is helpful to make short plot summaries of each scene so that students are aware of their characters' arcs throughout the play. The scene descriptions in the Folger editions are sufficient to fill in the plot holes. Students can read the descriptions aloud during class time to ensure that the story is clear and that no plot elements are neglected. Additionally, there are one-page charts in the Folger editions of *Shakespeare Set Free,* indicating characters' relations graphically, with lines connecting families and factions to give students a visual representation of what can often be complex interrelationships, particularly in Shakespeare's history plays.

Young actors love action. That is why *The 30-Minute Shakespeare* includes dynamic blocking (stage direction) that allows students to tell the story in a physically dramatic fashion. Characters' movements on the stage are always motivated by the text itself.

CHARACTER

I consider myself a facilitator and a director more than an acting teacher. I want the students' understanding of their characters to spring from the text and the story. From there, I encourage them to consider how their character might talk, walk, stand, sit, eat, and drink. I also urge students to consider characters' motivations, objectives, and relationships, and I will ask pointed questions to that end during the rehearsal process. I try not to show the students how I would perform a scene, but if no ideas are forthcoming from anybody in the class, I will suggest a minimum of two possibilities for how the character might respond.

At times students may want more guidance and examples. Over thirteen years of directing plays in the classroom, I have wavered between wanting all the ideas to come from the students, and deciding that I need to be more of a "director," telling them what I would like to see them doing. It is a fine line, but in recent years I have decided that if I don't see enough dynamic action or characterization, I will step in and "direct" more. But I always make sure to leave room for students to bring themselves into the characters because their own ideas are invariably the best.

THEME (THOUGHTS, IDEAS)

In a typical English classroom, theme will be a big topic for discussion of a Shakespeare play. Using a performance-based method of teaching Shakespeare, an understanding of the play's themes develops from "mining the text" and exploring Shakespeare's words and his story. If the students understand what they are saying and how that relates to their characters and the overall story, the plays' themes will emerge clearly. We always return to the text itself. There are a number of elegant computer programs, such as www.wordle.net, that will count the number of recurring words in a passage and illustrate them graphically. For example, if the word "jealousy" comes up more than any other word in *Othello,* it will appear in a larger font. Seeing the words displayed by size in this way can offer up illuminating insights into the interaction between words in the text and the play's themes. Your computer-minded students might enjoy searching for such tidbits. There are more internet tools and websites in the Additional Resources section at the back of this book.

I cannot overstress the importance of acting out the play in understanding its themes. By embodying the roles of Othello and Iago and reciting their words, students do not simply comprehend the themes intellectually, but understand them kinesthetically, physically, and emotionally. They are essentially *living* the characters' jealousy, pride, and feelings about race. The themes of appearance vs.

reality, good vs. evil, honesty, misrepresentation, and self-knowledge (or lack thereof) become physically felt as well as intellectually understood. Performing Shakespeare delivers a richer understanding than that which comes from just reading the play. Students can now relate the characters' conflicts to their own struggles.

DICTION (LANGUAGE)

If I had to cite one thing I would like my actors to take from their experience of performing a play by William Shakespeare, it is an appreciation and understanding of the beauty of Shakespeare's language. The language is where it all begins and ends. Shakespeare's stories are dramatic, his characters are rich and complex, and his settings are exotic and fascinating, but it is through his language that these all achieve their richness. This leads me to spend more time on language than on any other element of the performance.

Starting with daily vocal warm-ups, many of them using parts of the script or other Shakespearean passages, I consistently emphasize the importance of the words. Young actors often lack experience in speaking clearly and projecting their voices outward, so in addition to comprehension, I emphasize projection, diction, breathing, pacing, dynamics, coloring of words, and vocal energy. *Theatre Games for Young Performers* contains many effective vocal exercises, as does the Folger's *Shakespeare Set Free* series. Consistent emphasis on all aspects of Shakespeare's language, especially on how to speak it effectively, is the most important element to any Shakespeare performance with a young cast.

MUSIC

A little music can go a long way in setting a mood for a thirty-minute Shakespeare play. I usually open the show with a short passage of music to set the tone. Thirty seconds of music played on a boom box operated by a student can provide a nice introduction to the play, create an atmosphere for the audience, and give the actors a sense of place and feeling.

iTunes is a good starting point for choosing your music. Typing in "Shakespeare" or "Hamlet" or "jealousy" (if you are going for a theme) will result in an excellent selection of aural performance enhancers at the very reasonable price of ninety-nine cents each (or free of charge, see Additional Resources section). Likewise, fight sounds, foreboding sounds, weather sounds (rain, thunder), trumpet sounds, etc. are all readily available online at affordable cost. I typically include three sound cues in a play, just enough to enhance but not overpower a production. The boom box operator sits on the far right or left of the stage, not backstage, so he can see the action. This also has the added benefit of having somebody out there with a script, capable of prompting in a pinch.

SPECTACLE

Aristotle considered spectacle the least important aspect of drama. Students tend to be surprised at this since we are used to being bombarded with production values on TV and video, often at the expense of substance. In my early days of putting on student productions, I would find myself hamstrung by my own ambitions in the realm of scenic design.

A simple bench or two chairs set on the stage are sufficient. The sense of "place" can be achieved through language and acting. Simple set dressing, a few key props, and some tasteful, emblematic costume pieces will go a long way toward providing all the "spectacle" you need.

In the stage directions to the plays in *The 30-Minute Shakespeare* series, I make frequent use of two large pillars stage left and right at the Folger Shakespeare Library's Elizabethan Theatre. I also have characters frequently entering and exiting from "stage rear." Your stage will have a different layout. Take a good look at the performing space you will be using and see if there are any elements that can be incorporated into your own stage directions. Is there a balcony? Can characters enter from the audience? (Make sure that they can get there from backstage, unless you want them waiting in the lobby until their entrance, which may be impractical.) If possible, make sure to rehearse in that space a few times to fix any technical issues and perhaps discover a few fun staging variations that will add pizzazz and dynamics to your own show.

The real spectacle is in the telling of the tale. Wooden swords are handy for characters that need them. Students should be warned at the outset that playing with swords outside of the scene is verboten. Letters, moneybags, and handkerchiefs should all have plentiful duplicates kept in a small prop box, as well as with a stage manager, because they tend to disappear in the hands of adolescents. After every rehearsal and performance, I recommend you personally sweep the rehearsal or performance area immediately for stray props. It is amazing what gets left behind.

Ultimately, the performances are about language and human drama, not set pieces, props, and special effects. Fake blood, glitter, glass, and liquids have no place on the stage; they are a recipe for disaster, or, at the very least, a big mess. On the other hand, the props that are employed can often be used effectively to convey character, as in Bardolph's aforementioned relationship with his wineskin.

PITFALLS AND SOLUTIONS

Putting on a play in a high school classroom is not easy. There are problems with enthusiasm, attitude, attention, and line memorization, to name a few. As anybody who has directed a play will tell you, it is always darkest before the dawn. My experience is that after one or two days of utter despair just before the play goes up, show day breaks and the play miraculously shines. To quote a recurring gag in one of my favorite movies, *Shakespeare in Love*: "It's a mystery."

ENTHUSIASM, FRUSTRATION, AND DISCIPLINE

Bring the enthusiasm yourself. Feed on the energy of the eager students, and others will pick up on that. Keep focused on the task at hand. Arrive prepared. Enthusiasm comes as you make headway. Ultimately, it helps to remind the students that a play is fun. I try to focus on the positive attributes of the students, rather than the ones that drive me crazy. This is easier said than done, but it is important. One season, I yelled at the group two days in a row. On day two of yelling, they tuned me out, and it took me a while to win them back. I learned my lesson; since then I've tried not to raise my voice out of anger or frustration. As I grow older and more mature, it is important for me to lead by example. It has been years since I yelled at a student group. If I am disappointed in their work or their behavior, I will express my disenchantment in words, speaking from the heart as somebody who cares about them and cares about our performance and our experience together. I find that fundamentally, young people want to please, to do well, and to be liked. If there is a serious discipline problem, I will hand it over to the regular classroom teacher, the administrator, or the parent.

LINE MEMORIZATION

Students may have a hard time memorizing lines. In these cases, see if you can pair them up with a "buddy" and existing friend who will run lines with them in person or over the phone after school. If students do not have such a "buddy," I volunteer to run lines with them myself. If serious line memorization problems arise that cannot be solved through work, then two students can switch parts if it is early enough in the rehearsal process. For doubled roles, the scene with fewer lines can go to the actor who is having memorization problems. Additionally, a few passages or lines can be cut. Again, it is important to address these issues early. Later cuts become more problematic as other actors have already memorized their cues. I have had to do late cuts about twice in thirteen years. While they have gotten us out of jams, it is best to assess early whether a student will have line memorization problems, and deal with the problem sooner rather than later.

In production, always keep several copies of the script backstage, as well as cheat sheets indicating cues, entrances, and scene changes. Make a prop list, indicating props for each scene, as well as props that are the responsibility of individual actors. Direct the Stage Manager and an Assistant Stage Manager to keep track of these items, and on show days, personally double-check if you can.

In thirteen years of preparing an inner-city public high school English class for a public performance on a field trip to the Folger Secondary School Shakespeare Festival, my groups and I have been beset by illness, emotional turmoil, discipline problems, stage fright, adolescent angst, midlife crises (not theirs), and all manner of other emergencies, including acts of God and nature. Despite the difficulties and challenges inherent in putting on a Shakespeare play with a group of young people, one amazing fact stands out in my experience. Here is how many times a student has been absent for show day: Zero. Somehow, everybody has always made it to the show, and the show has gone on. How can this be? It's a mystery.

✳ PERFORMANCE NOTES: *MACBETH*

For young actors, there is a delicious joy in conjuring the evil that pervades *Macbeth*. Against a backdrop of "fog and filthy air," the play not only gives us a wealth of bloody deeds, but also their psychic consequences. This thirty-minute version of "The Scottish Play" offers us an opportunity to mine Shakespeare's text for all the poetic horror it offers. Once you have played in *Macbeth*, you may never be the same again.

I directed this performance of *Macbeth* in 2008. These notes are the result of my own review of the performance video. They are not intended to be the "definitive" performance notes for all productions of Macbeth. Your production will be unique to you and your cast. That is the magic of live theater. What is interesting about these notes is that many of the performance details I mention were not part of the original stage directions. They either emerged spontaneously on performance day or were developed by students in rehearsal after the stage directions had been written into the script. Some of these pieces of stage business work like a charm. Others fall flat. Still others are unintentionally hilarious. My favorites are the ones that arise directly from the students themselves, and demonstrate a union between actor and character, as if that individual becomes a vehicle for the character she is playing. To witness a seventeen-year-old young woman "become" Macbeth as Shakespeare's words leave her mouth is a memorable moment indeed.

In this particular production of *Macbeth*, two of my Three Witches had serious attitude problems. I wish I could have translated or transformed their anger into acting, but because their anger manifested itself by their acting bored, it showed in their performances. Their physical demeanor was so casual, it was as if they were not onstage at all.

This is rare. Most young actors who appear casual and nonchalant during the rehearsal period rise to the acting occasion on show day, and some even undergo radical transformations. But not these Witches. As a result, our play opens on a strangely un-mysterious note, featuring indifferent, blasé characters.

As director, I blame myself. In retrospect I should have gotten help from someone with dance experience to teach the actors more specific choreography. The actors playing the Witches had mentioned that they were cheerleaders. With better dance choreography and more specific physical directions, they might have had more fun, and dynamic movement might have usurped their bored physical countenance. It is also possible that working with a second adult could have increased their chances of responding positively to directions.

SCENE 1 (ACT I, SCENES I AND II)

I incorporate a "scarf dance" into the Witches' movements at the top of the scene, which works nicely, but afterward Second Witch continually fiddles with her scarf while other action is happening onstage. I mention this specifically several times in rehearsal, but on performance day, the fidgeting continues. It is a tough dynamic for a director, especially in this case, since we have only one public performance and therefore no second chances to iron out what has not been fixed in rehearsals.

I continue to give the actors notes up until performance day, because it is my job to ensure that we are as prepared as possible to give our best performance. Once the show opens, it is out of my hands. It is their play.

Fortunately, for every bored Witch, there is an animated Macbeth. In Scene 1, a young lady plays Macbeth with enough amazement and excitement at the Witches' news to mitigate their aforementioned torpor, thus saving the first scene!

SCENE 2 (ACT I, SCENES IV AND V)

The same scene-saving Macbeth from Scene 1 brings crisp gestures and strong diction to Scene 2. What ultimately sells character and story to an audience is personal commitment to the role, to the person portrayed, his words, emotions, and relationships. This becomes a commitment to bringing to life the story we are telling as a group.

Although very short, Scene 2 is actually a combination of Act I, Scenes IV and V. Combining scenes is a good technique to advance the plot quickly without the interruption of a scene change. Both scenes concern Macbeth's ambition, so fusing them makes sense. The actor playing Macbeth should have fun, as we see the dark ambition spread over his face and express itself through his poetic words.

A student I first worked with when he was a ninth grader, now a senior, plays King Duncan in this production. Memorizing even a few lines was a challenge for him, and it made him very nervous. I had run lines with him over the phone for the earlier play, *Romeo and Juliet,* and I did so again for *Macbeth.* It helped a lot. The most rewarding aspect of this project can be when the process of preparing for and performing a play brings confidence and pride in accomplishment to students who may have learning disabilities or other challenges that make school an anxiety-provoking experience for them.

SCENE 3 (ACT II, SCENES I AND II)

I love it when students have a naturally dynamic vocal instrument that they discover through acting. This was the case with the actress playing Lady Macbeth in this powerful scene. Lady Macbeth's voice on, "Come you spirits that tend on mortal thoughts, unsex me here," is delivered with a chilling clarity, piercing to the back row of the balcony.

For the "Is this a dagger I see before me?" speech, Macbeth begins the speech sitting, facing forward, and then rises and walks downstage following the dagger. The speech should intensify, and the movements should be motivated by the text. For example, Macbeth stands on, "Come, let me clutch thee," and sets off in pursuit of the dagger.

In this performance, after the line, "The very stones prate of my whereabouts," there should have been an offstage bell ring. That cue did not arrive, so the actress playing Macbeth gave a long pause, and then repeated the line more insistently, to some laughter from the audience. There was a longer pause, as the bell still did not ring. It was clear to me that a bell ringing was not imminent, so I clapped my hands twice from the audience, and Macbeth continued with his next line.

I try to instill this general principle upon young actors: If a cue, whether onstage or offstage, does not appear to be forthcoming, *keep going!* Macbeth has excellent theatrical momentum in the dagger speech, but it was disrupted and dissipated by delay and laughter due to a botched sound cue. Botched sound cues may be inevitable; therefore one must preemptively prepare a response. If Macbeth had cocked his ear and *acted as if* he heard a bell, the scene could have continued seamlessly. Not only is "mime hearing" a good acting exercise, but also, in the context of the story itself, if Macbeth can hallucinate a dagger, he can just as easily hallucinate a bell!

A prop, such as a dagger, is a good pointing tool, one that summons Macbeth to heaven *(point upward with dagger)* or to hell *(point downward with dagger)*. Simple stage directions give the actor a starting point for physicalizations. They set the wheels in motion, opening up new spontaneous physicalizations in rehearsal that may end up as part of the performance.

The pacing is important in this scene. Just as the dagger speech increases in urgency as it continues, so the scene itself become more desperate. Each sound (a knock, a bell, an owl) intensifies Macbeth and Lady Macbeth's terror and brings the scene to its panicked peak.

SCENE 4 (ACT V, SCENE IV)

This Scene, featuring Banquo's ghost, is notoriously tricky to stage. We make the choice to have Banquo sit at the table with his back to the audience, and at the appropriate moments, slowly rise and point at Macbeth. Rather than apply gruesome makeup and fake blood, we allow the horror in Macbeth's imagination to paint a fearsome picture for the audience. If possible, Banquo's stool should be shorter than the table chairs to avoid blocking the other actors seated at the table.

By focusing on the impact of Shakespeare's words rather than cluttering the story with props and makeup, the true horror of the story reveals itself through Shakespeare's powerful text and the strong imagination and conviction the young actors bring to their characters.

SCENE 5 (ACT IV, SCENE I)

Entrances are important. Young actors tend to amble onto the stage. In this scene, the Three Witches do just that. They appear pedestrian as they enter, and when they put the ingredients ("eye of newt," etc.) into the boiling cauldron, they look as if they are shuffling through their purses for lipstick. The Witches' entrance should be mysterious, evil, and intriguing. Next time, I will enlist the help of a choreographer to help add these elements to the Witches' movements. Sometimes I stubbornly think I can direct all aspects of the performance, but the truth is that I can use help.

The blocking in this scene is effective if First Witch stands stage right, Second Witch stands stage left, and Third Witch kneels downstage center. This way, when Macbeth stands center stage, the Witches surround him. Then when the pre-recorded thunder plays, Macbeth responds by looking up and all around him as if the noise is coming from different places. And every time he turns around, there is another Witch facing him! In this way the sounds and physical blocking reinforce the idea that Macbeth is being entrapped.

The Witches' exit should echo their entrance. They should leave the stage with energy and evil intent. One solution to the problem of ambling entrances is to have the actors recite their lines while they are coming onstage so that they enter in character, rather than waiting until they are fully onstage before speaking.

SCENE 6 (ACT V, SCENE I)

In this chilling scene, Lady Macbeth wanders in her sleep, while her Gentlewoman and the Doctor look on in shocked amazement. The actor playing Lady Macbeth has a good opportunity to go beyond the limits of normal human behavior. Lady Macbeth is essentially walking in a living nightmare. She has previously been brutally unrepentant, but now her unconscious rises and expresses itself as she tries desperately to rub out the "damned spot."

The actor should wander with open eyes, but not focus on the two observers. Her voice should be markedly different from her waking voice. She should experiment with higher and lower pitches, and sing-songy cadences. While rehearsing this scene, I continually encourage the actor to take some risks and try to push the character's words and actions to a place where they will frighten the audience. The effect should be visceral.

It is challenging to achieve the proper level of emotional intensity with young actors because they are hesitant to embarrass themselves. Sometimes I will stop the scene and have the entire group recite a speech together, starting at a low volume and ending up practically screaming. There is safety in numbers, and when the whole group risks taking the energy to a higher level, the individual is freer to do the same.

SCENE 7 (ACT V, SCENE VIII)

Thanks to the assistance of my annual fight choreography resource, Michael Tolaydo, this production ends on a strong note, with the climactic fight between Macbeth and Macduff. I feel very grateful to have the help of a seasoned professional in matters where I lack experience and expertise. I urge anyone who is putting on a Shakespeare show with young people to seek out qualified helpers in areas such as voice, dance, music, and combat from your own circle of colleagues. We adults tend to work independently, which is handy, but only up to a point. There are people nearby who will gladly offer their talents. As an added benefit, it expands your personal and professional network. Sometimes it takes a village to build a Shakespeare play.

In this version of the scene, a woman plays Macbeth and a man depicts Macduff. It is gratifying to have intergender fighting in a clash normally enacted by two men. This type of non-traditional casting can shed new light on a scene. It adds a nice modern touch to this classic battle, and the women in both the cast and the audience seem to appreciate it.

The actual killing of Macbeth happens offstage in this production. Macduff re-enters with a slightly deflated volleyball in a sack, which adequately represents a severed head. Of course you have the option of purchasing or manufacturing a severed head prop, but the danger is that this might elicit laughter rather than horror. Still, if somebody in your group feels he or she can make a stab at building a dead head, by all means encourage this. As with pieces of stage business, props and costumes made by cast members contribute to the feeling of ownership of the project, which adds to group unity and pride.

This play ends with the "Out, out brief candle" soliloquy (from Act V, Scene V), spoken in unison by the group. The actors begin the speech as they walk on stage, and by the time the speech ends, the whole ensemble is center stage with their voices rising. By the time they reach the concluding line, "Signifying nothing!" they are at a full shout, with arms upraised. They then hold hands and go into their triumphant bow. It is quite effective to take a dramatic passage from somewhere else in the script to end the play. It adds a memorable exclamation point to one of Shakespeare's memorable tragedy, one so steeped in mystery and horror that many actors dare not speak its name on the stage, referring to it only as "The Scottish Play."

Live theater is magical. It is the most dynamic form of entertainment available to us. There is nothing like the interchange between actors and audience, that vibrant energy that is created in the theater. *Macbeth* is surely one of the most powerful and enduring dramas ever written, and we are fortunate to be able to continue bringing it to life, especially with young performers who can give it the vitality it deserves.

✳ *MACBETH:*
SET AND PROP LIST

SET PIECES:

One throne

Four chairs

One table

PROPS

THROUGHOUT:

Swords

Crowns

SCENE 1:

Scarves for Witches

SCENE 3:

Letter

Two daggers

SCENE 4:

Mugs

SCENE 5:

Cauldron

Rubber ingredients for cauldron: entrails (finger, eye, liver, tongue, etc.), snakes, and so on

SCENE 7:

"Severed head" in bag (slightly deflated volleyball)

Macbeth

By William Shakespeare

Tuesday, March 11th, 2008
Senior English Class | Instructor: Mr Leo Bowman
Guest Director: Mr. Nick Newlin
Guest Fight Choreographer, Scene 7: Michael Tolaydo

CAST OF CHARACTERS:

SCENE 1
First Witch: Di'mond Spencer
2nd Witch: Faudilia Roca
3rd Witch: Porche' Spencer
Macbeth: Janay McPherson
Banquo: Charnita Rush
Ross: Nathan Acors

SCENE 2
Narrator: Jasmine Queen
Duncan: Muhammad Mack
Macbeth: Janay McPherson
Banquo: Charnita Rush
Malcom: Jasmine Wilson

SCENE 3
Narrator: Jasmine Dunn
Lady Macbeth: Jasmine Queen
Macbeth: Whitney Powell

SCENE 4
Narrator: Renee' Edelin
Macbeth: Whitney Powell
Ross: Nathan Acors
First Murderer: Shaunte' Canty
Lennox: Jasmine Wilson
Lady Macbeth: Kendra Allen
Banquo: Charnita Rush

SCENE 5
Narrator: Renee' Edelin
First Witch: Di'mond Spencer
2nd Witch: Faudilia Roca
3rd Witch: Porche' Spencer
Macbeth: Jasmine Dunn
Lennox: Jasmine Wilson

SCENE 6
Narrator: Jasmine Queen
Gentlewoman: Renee' Edelin
Doctor: Charnita Rush
Lady Macbeth: Kendra Allen

SCENE 7
Narrator: Jasmine Queen
Macbeth: Jasmine Dunn
Macduff: Devin Newton
Malcom: Janay McPherson

Stage Manager: Jasmine Dunn
Sound: Muhammad Mack

Come, thick night,
And pall thee in the dunnest smoke of hell,
That my keen knife see not the wound it makes,
Nor heaven peep through the blanket of the dark,
to cry "Hold, hold!"
—Lady Macbeth

ADDITIONAL RESOURCES

SHAKESPEARE

Shakespeare Set Free: Teaching Romeo and Juliet, Macbeth and a Midsummer Night's Dream
Peggy O'Brien, Ed., Teaching Shakespeare Institute
Washington Square Press
New York, 1993

Shakespeare Set Free: Teaching Hamlet and Henry IV, Part 1
Peggy O'Brien, Ed., Teaching Shakespeare Institute
Washington Square Press
New York, 1994

Shakespeare Set Free: Teaching Twelfth Night and Othello
Peggy O'Brien, Ed., Teaching Shakespeare Institute
Washington Square Press
New York, 1995

The *Shakespeare Set Free* series is an invaluable resource with lesson plans, activites, handouts, and excellent suggestions for rehearsing and performing Shakespeare plays in a classroom setting.

ShakesFear and How to Cure It!
Ralph Alan Cohen
Prestwick House, Inc.
Delaware, 2006

The Friendly Shakespeare:
A Thoroughly Painless Guide
to the Best of the Bard
Norrie Epstein
Penguin Books
New York, 1994

Brush Up Your Shakespeare!
Michael Macrone
Cader Books
New York, 1990

Shakespeare's Insults:
Educating Your Wit
Wayne F. Hill and Cynthia J. Ottchen
Three Rivers Press
New York, 1991

Practical Approaches to
Teaching Shakespeare
Peter Reynolds
Oxford University Press
New York, 1991

Scenes From Shakespeare:
A Workbook for Actors
Robin J. Holt
McFarland and Co.
London, 1988

THEATER AND PERFORMANCE

Impro: Improvisation and the Theatre
Keith Johnstone
Routledge Books
London, 1982

A Dictionary of Theatre Anthropology:
The Secret Art of the Performer
Eugenio Barba and Nicola Savarese
Routledge
London, 1991

THEATER GAMES

Theatre Games for Young Performers
Maria C. Novelly
Meriwether Publishing
Colorado, 1990

Improvisation for the Theater
Viola Spolin
Northwestern University Press
Illinois, 1983

Theater Games for Rehearsal:
A Director's Handbook
Viola Spolin
Northwestern University Press
Illinois, 1985

101 Theatre Games for Drama
Teachers, Classroom Teachers
& Directors
Mila Johansen
Players Press Inc.
California, 1994

PLAY DIRECTING

Theater and the Adolescent Actor:
Building a Successful School Program
Camille L. Poisson
Archon Books
Connecticut, 1994

Directing for the Theatre
W. David Sievers
Wm. C. Brown, Co.
Iowa, 1965

The Director's Vision: Play Direction
from Analysis to Production
Louis E. Catron
Mayfield Publishing Co.
California, 1989

INTERNET RESOURCES

http://www.folger.edu
The Folger Shakespeare Library's website has lesson plans, primary sources, study guides, images, workshops, programs for teachers and students, and much more. The definitive Shakespeare website for educators, historians and all lovers of the Bard.

http://www.shakespeare.mit.edu.
The Complete Works of
William Shakespeare.
All complete scripts for *The 30-Minute Shakespeare* series were originally downloaded from this site before editing. Links to other internet resources.

http://www.LoMonico.com/Shakespeare-and-Media.htm
http://shakespeare-and-media.wikispaces.com
Michael LoMonico is Senior Consultant on National Education for the Folger Shakespeare Library. His *Seminar Shakespeare 2.0* offers a wealth of information on how to use exciting new approaches and online resources for teaching Shakespeare.

http://www.freesound.org.
A collaborative database of sounds and sound effects.

http://www.wordle.net.
A program for creating "word clouds" from the text that you provide. The clouds give greater prominence to words that appear more frequently in the source text.

http://www.opensourceshakespeare.org.
This site has good searching capacity.

http://shakespeare.palomar.edu/default.htm
Excellent links and searches

http://shakespeare.com/
Write like Shakespeare, Poetry Machine, tag cloud

http://www.shakespeare-online.com/

http://www.bardweb.net/

http://www.rhymezone.com/shakespeare/
Good searchable word and phrase finder.
Or by lines:
http://www.rhymezone.com/shakespeare/toplines/

http://shakespeare.mcgill.ca/
Shakespeare and Performance research team

http://www.enotes.com/william-shakespeare

Needless to say, the internet goes on and on with valuable Shakespeare resources. The ones listed here are excellent starting points and will set you on your way in the great adventure that is Shakespeare.

NICK NEWLIN has performed a comedy and variety act for international audiences for twenty-seven years. Since 1996, he has conducted an annual play directing residency affiliated with the Folger Shakespeare Library in Washington, D.C. Newlin received a BA with Honors from Harvard University in 1982 and an MA in Theater with an emphasis in Play Directing from the University of Maryland in 1996.

THE 30-MINUTE SHAKESPEARE

A MIDSUMMER NIGHT'S DREAM
978-1-935550-00-6

AS YOU LIKE IT
978-1-935550-06-8

MUCH ADO ABOUT NOTHING
978-1-935550-03-7

THE COMEDY OF ERRORS
978-1-935550-08-2

THE MERRY WIVES OF WINDSOR
978-1-935550-05-1

HENRY IV, PART 1
978-1-935550-11-2

ROMEO AND JULIET
978-1-935550-01-3

LOVE'S LABOR'S LOST
978-1-935550-07-5

MACBETH
978-1-935550-02-0

KING LEAR
978-1-935550-09-9

TWELFTH NIGHT
978-1-935550-04-4

OTHELLO
978-1-935550-10-5

All plays $7.95, available in bookstores everywhere

"*Nick Newlin's 30-minute play cuttings are perfect for students who have no experience with Shakespeare. Each 30-minute mini-play is a play in itself with a beginning, middle, and end.*" —Michael Ellis-Tolaydo, Department of Theater, Film, and Media Studies, St Mary's College of Maryland

PHOTOCOPYING AND PERFORMANCE RIGHTS